Sewing Machine Repair
For The Home Sewer

Reuben O. Doyle

ISBN-13: 978-0615592138
ISBN-10: 0615592139

DEDICATION

I would like to dedicate this book to my wife, Sarah. Without her encouragement and support this book would not have been possible. And to our daughter, Denise, for painstakingly editing and typesetting the book.

CONTENTS

INTRODUCTION

As a sewing machine repairman for over 25 years, I have seen just about every problem that can happen with a sewing machine.

I've seen people so frustrated with knotted thread, breaking needles, and thread that won't pick up from the bobbin that they'd like to lock their machine up in a closet and forget they ever had one!

The sad part of this total frustration is that in many cases, the "problem" is so minor (needle in backwards or the like) that if the home sewer had known what to look for and what minor adjustments to make, the problem could have been solved long before the frustration set in. Granted, major machine repair problems such as broken machine parts need to be taken to an authorized service center for repair, but in at least 75% of the service calls I've made, the home sewer could have easily handled the problem on their own if they had a little information.

This book is written for those sewing machine problems that fall into the 75% category that can be easily taken care of by the home sewer. We'll show you what to look for, how to check for tension adjustments, and numerous other hints and tips to make sewing the pleasurable and fun hobby it was meant to be!

1 BASIC PARTS AND CONTROLS

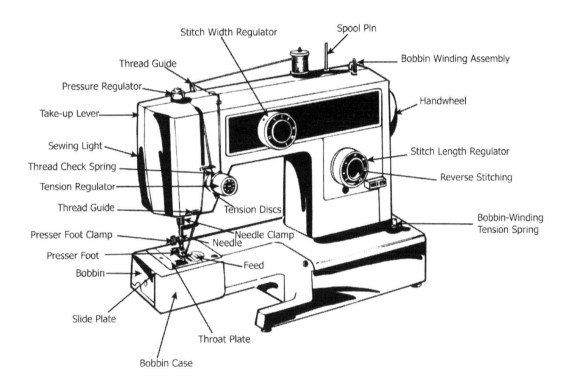

There are dozens of sewing machines on the market today, each one emphasizing what they do that other ones cannot do. In addition, there are hundreds of older models that are in homes and sewing shops all over the country.

With the emphasis on the differences, it is sometimes easy to forget that sewing machines are all basically similar. All of the operating parts that are labeled on the machine on this page are common to any average machine that will do both straight and zig zag stitching. The position of some of these items may differ and be placed somewhat differently on some machines, but all of the parts are there.

The basic requirement of all the various sewing machine brands is a precisely timed movement of the needle and shuttle hook to manipulate the top and bottom (bobbin) thread to make a stitch. The method the machines use to make the stitches is shown in figure 101:

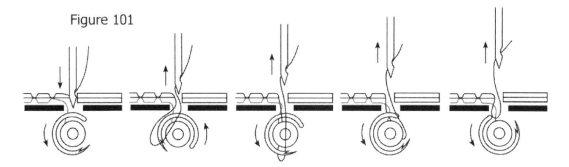

Figure 101

1) The needle penetrates the fabric to take the top thread into the bobbin area.

2) As the needle rises, the top thread forms a loop for the shuttle hook to catch.

3) The shuttle hook carries the thread loop around and under the bobbin case.

4) The loop slides off the hook and bobbin case, and goes around the bobbin thread.

5) The threads are pulled up and are set into the fabric as a lockstitch.

Because of the similarities between all sewing machines on the market, it is possible to write a sewing machine repair manual that applies to all machines.

The instructions written throughout this book are general in nature and apply to any type or brand of sewing machine, however there may be an exception to some of the instructions because there are hundreds of different makes and models of sewing machines made all over the world.

To create a book of this type, usable by anyone who owns a sewing machine, it is necessary to write in general terms. If there is an exception, and our suggestion to a particular problem does not seem to work on your machine, please refer to your sewing machine's operational manual - the manufacturer's instruction manual will take precedence in that case. If the problem you're experiencing is due to a broken part, a worn gear that needs to be replaced, or something along those lines, you will need to take the machine to an authorized service center for repair.

The sewing machine problems addressed throughout this book are ones dealing with threads, tensions, fabric problems, cleaning and maintenance, which covers over 75% of the problems experienced by home sewers and crafters.

2 SEWING MACHINE SKIPS STITCHES

1) Needle inserted improperly.

A. The flat side of the needle must face the shaft (see figure 102).

B. The groove in the needle faces away from the shaft; (this applies to needles that are round, with no flat side (see figure 102).

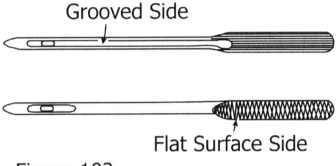

Grooved Side

Flat Surface Side

Figure 102

Correct needle insertion is mandatory for the proper use of your sewing machine. Raise the needle bar to the highest point, then loosen the clamp screw to remove the old needle. Place the new needle in the clamp with the **flat side of the needle facing the back** (or if using a round needle, the groove in the needle should face away from the shaft). Push the needle all the way up to the stop, or as far as it will go, then tighten the needle clamp screw (figure 103).

Figure 103

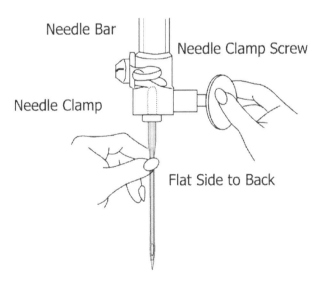

Needle Bar

Needle Clamp Screw

Needle Clamp

Flat Side to Back

Changing the Needle

2) Possible bent needle - lay the needle on a flat surface and roll the needle over. If the needle does not roll true, then it is bent and needs to be replaced.

3) Blunt needle point - if the needle makes a popping sound when the needle penetrates the fabric, the needle point is blunt and should be replaced.

4) Needle is not all the way up in holder —loosen needle clamp screw and push the needle up until it stops; tighten clamp screw.

5) Incorrect threading - check your instruction manual for proper threading of your sewing machine. It only takes one missed step in the sequence of threading to cause your machine to skip stitches.

6) Wrong needle for your machine - Check your instruction manual for the proper needle for the make and model number of your particular machine. Some machines can use a generic type of needle with no problem; however, some machines require the specific ones mentioned in the instruction manual.

7) Size of needle and thread not compatible – Sometimes people get in too much of a hurry to start on the next sewing or craft project and they don't take the time to make sure they're using the correct needle and thread for the fabric type. When using the wrong type of needle for the job, the end result likely won't be what you expected, and could possibly cause stitching problems throughout the project. A needle too fine for heavy fabric can bend or break when it hits the fabric, while too large a needle for fine fabric can make puncture holes in the material and also cause the thread to pull unevenly while stitching. The best practice is to check before beginning a project to make sure you're using the right fabric/thread/needle combinations (refer to chart in the back of this book).

3 MACHINE DOES NOT STITCH PROPERLY

1) Tensions are incorrect - the first thing you will want to check if the machine isn't making stitches correctly is whether both the upper and lower tensions are adjusted properly. Remove the bobbin case from the shuttle, and then remove the shuttle from the shuttle carrier. Put the bobbin case and shuttle together (figure #104). Hold the whole assembly by the thread (figure #104) and shake gently. If the bobbin case and shuttle slide down the thread very fast, then turn the adjusting screw clockwise to tighten. If the bobbin case and shuttle will not slide down the thread at all you will need to loosen the adjusting screw counter-clockwise until the bobbin and shuttle slide down a little, but stop sliding when you stop gently shaking the thread. This procedure works on nearly every sewing machine.

Figure 104

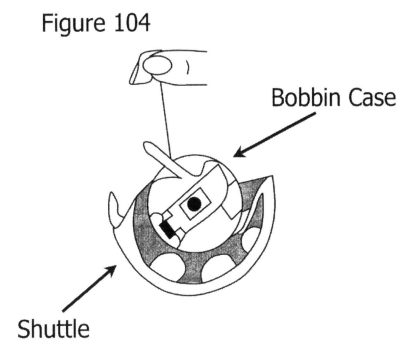

Bobbin Case

Shuttle

Now that you have the lower tension adjusted properly, put the shuttle back into the shuttle carrier of the sewing machine then put the bobbin case back into the shuttle. Once you have adjusted your lower tension following the previous instructions, some minor adjustment of your upper tension may be necessary to obtain the proper tension for your sewing machine. Find some scrap material and sew a few inches to determine what you'll need to do to finalize your upper tension adjustment. Adjust your upper tension until your thread ties off as shown in Figure 105 sample "A" below:

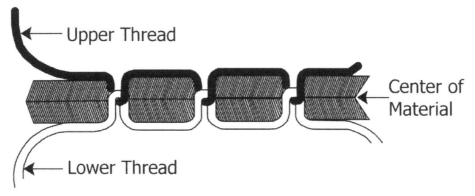

Figure 105A - Correct Tension

If your stitching looks like sample "B", the upper tension is too tight, and if it looks like sample "C", the lower tension is too tight We recommend that you use a different color of thread on top than in the bobbin so that you can easily see how your stitching line looks on the fabric.

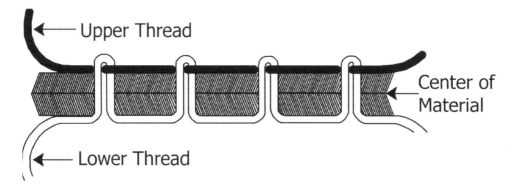

Figure 105B - Upper Tension Too Tight

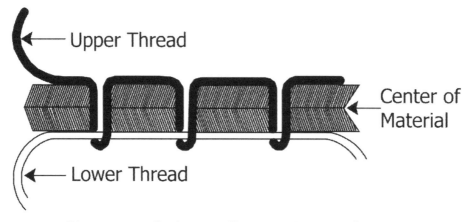

Figure 105C - Lower Tension Too Tight

NOTE: In most cases you will not have to adjust your lower tension. However, if you cannot get the upper tension to adjust properly, then and only then should you adjust your lower tension according to the instructions on the previous page.

As you change fabrics and begin sewing on different weight materials, test sew on a piece of scrap material of the same weight before you begin the actual sewing project so that you can adjust your upper tension for that particular material.

As an example, if you're changing from a denim type material to a silk or stretch knit type material, you would definitely want to make sure the tension is correct and the stitching looks correct before you start to sew on the garment.

To determine whether the upper tension is too tight or too loose for the fabric you're planning to sew, try the following test. Take a small square scrap of the fabric, fold it into a triangle, and stitch a line on the bias of the fabric using different colors of thread in the bobbin and on top. Grasp the bias line of stitching between your thumb and index finger. Space your hands about 3 inches apart and pull with an even, quick force until one thread breaks. If the broken thread is the color of the thread in the needle, it means that the upper tension is too tight. If the broken thread is the color of the bobbin thread, the upper tension is too loose. If both threads break together and take more force to break, it means that the tensions are balanced (figure 106).

Figure 106

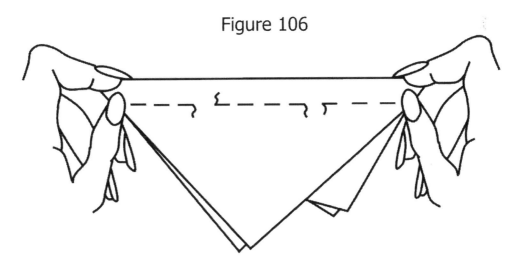

2) Stitches are ragged - this problem most likely will happen when two different sizes of thread are being used. Make sure to use the same thread in the bobbin as on the spool and never mix different sizes of thread. (The exception to this rule is if you're doing sewing machine embroidery, where you might want to use a heavier thread on the top to get a certain effect for your embroidery project.)

3) Length of stitches is erratic - this happens if the feed dog is not at the right height. Refer to your sewing machine instruction manual for the adjustment of your feed dog. Presser bar adjustment might also need to be made. Check your machine manual, but in most cases the adjustment is a dial knob on top over the drop lever that lets down the presser foot. Other types include a press down adjustment knob, screw down, or sometimes a dial knob inside the sewing machine opening at the left end of the machine that encases the light bulb. The presser bar adjustment is very important when you change from lightweight material to a heavyweight material. The presser bar adjustment controls how fast or slow the feed dogs "walk" your material through the sewing area. The following diagram shows how each of the presser bar adjustments work, so you will be able to easily locate the type that you have on your machine (figure 107).

Figure 107

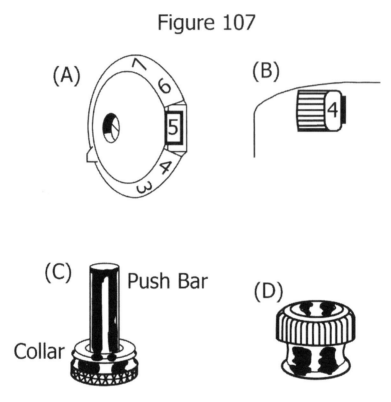

A. The dial on the side of the machine will either have numbers or words for the selection process. The words are self-explanatory. If your machine has numbers, the higher the number, the greater the pressure.

B. The dial on the top of the machine could also have either numbers or words. If the settings are words, they are usually "maximum", "minimum" or "darn".

C. The push bar regulator has a "lock-release" collar around it. When the bar is pushed down to increase the pressure, the collar locks the bar into place. When the collar is pushed, the bar is released and the pressure is decreased.

D. The screw type regulator is turned clockwise to increase the pressure, and counterclockwise to decrease the pressure.

The next diagram, figure 108, shows you what the pressure and feed area on the machine looks like, and how the various parts work together.

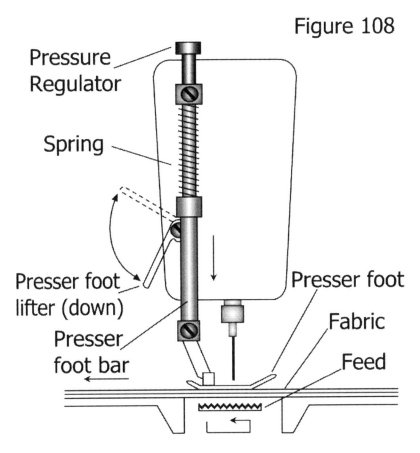

Figure 108

Pressure Regulator

Spring

Presser foot lifter (down)

Presser foot bar

Presser foot

Fabric

Feed

Pressure is the downward force that is placed on the fabric by the presser foot to hold the fabric layers taut in order that they might move together during the stitching process. The spring on the presser foot bar controls the amount of pressure applied. The pressure is changed through the use of the pressure regulator previously described and shown in figure 108. NOTE: The pressure on the presser foot can be changed only when the presser foot is in the "down" position.

Feed is the upward force that moves the fabric under the presser foot. The "stitch length" knob controls the feed. The shorter you have the stitch length set, the shorter the distance the feed moves the fabrics between each new stitch. The longer the stitch length is, the greater the distance between each new stitch. The following diagrams (figure 109) show how the feed and pressure work together to make the stitches.

Figure 109

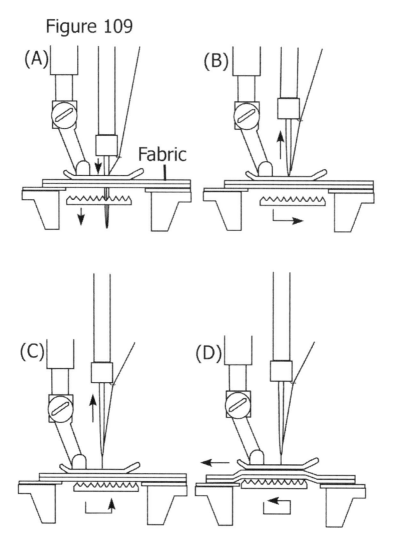

A. While the needle and thread penetrate the fabric, both the feed and presser foot hold the fabric taut. As the needle descends, the feed descends, leaving only the presser foot in contact with the fabric.

B. As the needle is coming up out of the fabric, the feed is moving forward. While this is happening, the presser foot continues to be in contact with the fabric.

C. As the needle continues to move upward and to bring the stitch with it, the feed is also moving up toward the fabric. The presser foot continues to hold the fabric.

D. As the stitch is being set into the fabric, the feed comes up to help the presser foot keep the fabric taut and then to advance the fabric one stitch length (the stitch length being regulated by the "stitch length" knob).

NOTE: Never pull your material through the sewing area! Let the feed dogs walk your material through naturally.

4) Stitches loose - loose stitches indicate a tension problem. Go back to the instructions for adjusting the tensions to correct this issue.

5) Thread loops on bottom - looping thread could be caused by two things - a blunt needle or a tension problem. Check the needle first. If it is even slightly rough or "blunt" at the tip, change the needle. Don't wait for a needle to actually break before changing it - many times stitching problems could be prevented altogether if a proper sharp needle is used. If the needle is okay, check the tension by using a scrap piece of material of the same weight as the sewing project, and refer back to the section on tension adjustments.

6) Frayed stitches - clean the machine of all lint in the lower bobbin assembly area. Also remove the feed dog (throat plate) in the needle area by removing the screw and lifting the plate off (figure 110) then brush out the lint inside that area.

7) Zig Zag stitches uneven - check the tension to correct this problem. Refer to the section on tension adjustment, and again, by using two different colors of thread you will be able to quickly see the tension adjustment that needs to be made.

Figure 110

4 SEWING MACHINE BREAKS UPPER THREAD

There are several possibilities why the machine breaks the upper thread. Use the following check list to see which is the problem in your particular instance:

1) Needle is in backwards - it is quite common for the sewer to either be unaware that there is a right and wrong way to insert a needle, or they may be in a hurry and mistakenly insert the needle the wrong way. In over 50% of my machine repair jobs the needle is in backwards, so this is definitely something to be aware of and always check first when having thread issues (refer to diagrams in Chapter 2).

2) The upper tension may be too tight - refer to the section on tensions in Chapter 3 to correct this.

3) The needle may be bent - try rolling the needle on a flat surface to see whether it is bent or not. If the needle is bent, replace it with a new one.

4) The thread may be hanging up on the bobbin case - check the bobbin case area for excess lint or fragments of old threads that need to be cleaned out.

5) Knotty or cheap thread is being used – always use a good quality thread for your sewing projects. The few cents that you save buying cheap thread could cost you big dollars on your sewing machine maintenance bill. Try holding a length of the cheap thread up to a lighted window and take a look at all the fuzz on it. The fuzziness causes a weakening in the thread that can cause the thread to break off more easily when it goes through the needle's eye and bobbin case, and it also creates a buildup of lint in your machine that can cause the machine to clog up and drag. This can result in many more maintenance issues than are necessary. Use the same 'window test' on good quality thread, look at the difference between the two types, then be sure to buy the better quality thread.

5 LOWER THREAD BREAKS

1) Improperly wound bobbin - the most probable cause of the lower thread breaking is an improperly' wound bobbin. Refer to your instruction book to find out exactly where to wind your bobbin. It may be the type that rewinds right in the machine, or maybe the winding mechanism is on the top near the hand wheel or on the front side near the hand wheel. Regardless of where you wind the bobbin, the basic rules apply to every type:

A. Always start with an empty bobbin. Never wind one color of thread over another color.

B. Choose thread that is identical in color and type as the one to be used for upper threading.

C. Wind the bobbin evenly across and in level layers. See figure 111 for the right and wrong way to wind a bobbin.

D. Don't wind the bobbin so full that it fits tightly and is hard to insert into the bobbin case. Most machines have an "automatic" shut off' when the bobbin gets full, but if yours does not, be careful not to let it fill too full.

Figure 111

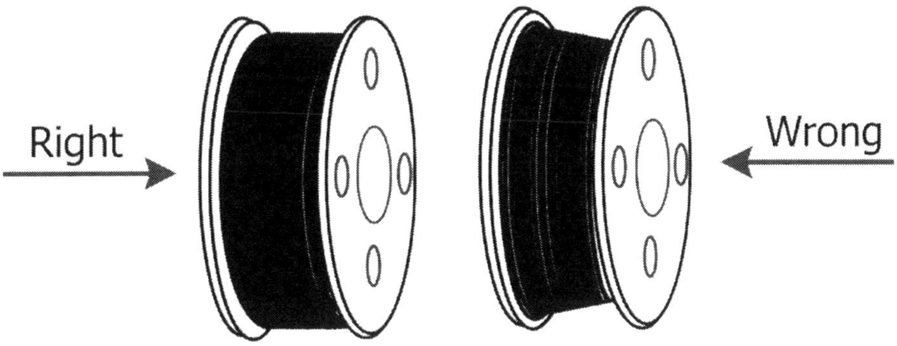

Right → ← Wrong

2) Bent bobbin - if the bobbin is bent then replace the bobbin with a new one and throw the old one away.

3) Lint build-up in the bobbin case – frequent cleanings will eliminate this problem. The more you use the sewing machine, the more often this area will need to be cleaned.

4) Thread catching on a spring or latch on the bobbin case - check to see that the bobbin is inserted completely and correctly, and that you are using the right kind of bobbin for your machine. If unsure, check your owner's manual for the type of bobbin you should use. Be sure to replace any bobbin that is worn, nicked or cracked as any type of damage to a bobbin can cause sewing problems. Keep several extras on hand to reduce downtime when a new one is needed. The following chart shows the various types of bobbins available (figure 112):

Figure 112

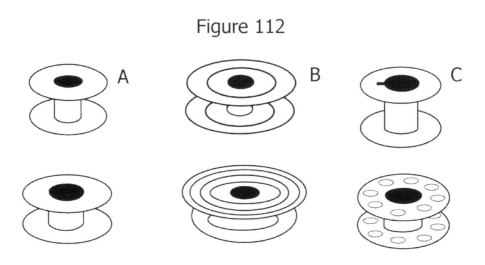

A. Most drop-in bobbins are made of plastic, but they can also be made of metal. They are smooth surfaced and the sides are usually rounder than other types of bobbins.

B. Special drop-in bobbins are made for those machines with the-winding mechanism built into the machine that allows you to rewind the bobbin without taking it out. This type of bobbin is made of clear plastic and the top half is sometimes larger than the bottom half. The top side also usually has circular lines indicating fullness of the bobbin.

C. Removable case bobbins may be made of plastic or metal. Their sides may be smooth surfaced, but some of the metal ones have several holes in each of the sides.

NOTE: *You may use generic type bobbins in addition to those made by your sewing machine manufacturer. Just make sure to purchase the same type as the ones pictured in your owner's manual.*

6 MACHINE BREAKS NEEDLES

1) Incorrect needle for machine - make sure you are using the right needle for your type of sewing machine. Most machines can use "generic" Schmetz needles; however, there are cases where the brand of machine will only use the variety specified in the owner's manual.

2) Presser foot - the presser foot may not be installed properly.

3) Incorrect needle for fabric - use the correct needle for the type of fabric you are working with; too fine a needle on heavy fabric or too coarse a needle on silky or jersey fabrics will cause problems. Refer to the "fabric/needle/thread" chart on the following page for assistance here.

4) Pulling the fabric through - the operator of the sewing machine may be pulling the fabric through the presser foot. Let the feed dogs guide the cloth through and under the presser foot to keep from putting undue pressure on the needle.

5) The needle is not all the way in - make sure the needle is set all the way up against the stop when you insert it before tightening the set screw.

FABRIC, THREAD, NEEDLE AND STITCH LENGTH CHART			
FABRICS	**THREAD SIZES**	**NEEDLE SIZES**	**STITCH LENGTH SETTING**
Delicate: Net, chiffon, silk, voile, fine lace, organdy	Fine mercerized "A" silk, synthetic	9	15 to 20
Lightweight: Batiste, synthetic, sheers, paper taffeta, silk, chiffon, velvet, stretch fabric, tricot, plastic film	50 mercerized "A" silk, synthetic	11	12 to 15 (8 to 10 for Plastic)
Medium weight: Gingham, pique, chambray, poplin, wool crepe, muslin, linen, chintz, double knit, jersey, flannel, wool, silk, fine corduroy, velveteen, satin, raw silk, wool suiting, drapery fabrics, stretch fabric	50 mercerized "A" silk 60 cotton Synthetic	14	12 to 15
Medium heavy: Denim, sail-cloth, gabardine, tweed, coatings, heavy suiting, stretch fabric, drapery fabrics	Heavy-Duty Mercerized "A" silk 40 to 60 cotton Synthetic	16	10 to 12
Heavy: Overcoatings, dungaree, ticking, canvas, upholstery fabrics	Heavy-duty Mercerized 24 to 50 cotton	18	8 to 10
All weights: Decorative top stitching	"D" silk ** buttonhole twist	18	6 to 12
**use with 50 mercerized or "A" silk in bobbin			

7 MACHINE WILL NOT FEED FABRIC THROUGH

1) The stitch adjustment control is set at "0" - adjust the stitch length to the proper "normal" setting.

2) Presser foot loose - check to make sure that the presser foot thumb screw is tight.

3) Feed dog position - the feed dog adjustment may be in the wrong position. Check to see that it is set to a raised position and not dropped down to the "darning" position.

4) Presser bar - the presser bar may not adjusted correctly. For thin material adjust to a little pressure on the foot; heavy fabric (denim, canvas, etc.) will need more pressure on the foot. Refer to Chapter 3 for presser bar adjustments if needed.

8 MACHINE WILL NOT RUN SMOOTHLY

1) Needs oil - the moving parts of the machine may need oiling. The simple way to know what to oil and where is "if it moves, oil it". Check your operating manual for a picture of the sewing machine and it should tell you where the locations are that need oil.

NOTE: Do not oil the electrical wiring or motor! Some older model motors have a location at each end for a drop of oil. Again, check the operating manual of your particular machine for specific oiling information.

2) Clogged bobbin area - lint and thread may be clogging the shuttle and hook assembly area (this is where your bobbin is located). Also check to see if lint and thread are jammed under the presser foot and feed dog area. Remove the screw holding the plate down and clean all of the lint and thread from this area. If your machine is used often then this area should be cleaned once a month; if it is used only once a week, then every three months should be often enough.

3) Out of alignment - if you just cleaned the shuttle and bobbin area, check that area again to see if something is now mis-aligned and is binding, causing your machine to run hard.

4) Belt is tight - if you have recently replaced a motor belt, it may be too tight. Adjust the belt so it will press together about half an inch or less (using the thumb and index finger). Try running the machine again; adjust again until your machine stops running hard.

CAUTION: If the motor belt is left too tight, it could burn out the motor, so it's better to have it a little loose than too tight.

5) Other belt issues - if you have checked all of the above issues but it still runs hard and your motor belt is located inside the machine, then it is best to take it to a dealer or authorized service repairman have it replaced.

9 MOTOR RUNS BUT THE MACHINE DOESN'T

1) Motor belt broken - the motor belt is very likely broken. You can replace the belt, but as previously mentioned, if the motor belt is located inside the machine, you should take it to an authorized service center for repair.

2) Motor belt loose - the motor belt may be loose. If so, adjust it so that the belt is tight, but not overly tight.

10 MOTOR DOES NOT RUN

1) Defective cord - check for any kinks or "bent" spots on the power cord. Even without visible evidence the electrical cord may be defective. If you suspect that could be the case, replace it with a new electrical cord.

2) Not plugged in - the electrical cord may have come unplugged from the wall socket (don't laugh, this happens more often than you might think!)

3) The motor may be burned out - smell the motor to see if it smells like a pair of dirty smelly socks. If the motor smells bad, it needs to be replaced.

4) Foot control not working - the foot control may be defective. The foot control may have stopped working, or if the foot control is partially burned out, the control will run at high speed only. If this is the case, and the foot control cord is permanently attached to the machine, you will need to take it to an authorized service repairman to be replaced. If the foot control for your machine is the plug-in type then you may also have the option of purchasing a replacement online. Search for the make and model of your machine plus the word "parts" in search engines, or visit eBay and search for the part there.

CAUTION: I recommend that you make it a habit to turn off the power and light switch before changing needles, presser feet or throat plates and when leaving the machine unattended. This will eliminate the possibility of a child or someone starting the sewing machine by accidentally pressing the speed control foot.

11 SHUTTLE SYSTEMS FOR SEWING MACHINES

There are three basic sewing mechanisms in the lockstitch category (Figure 113). The simplest type is the **"vibrator" (long shuttle) (A)**. These machines have a vibrator mechanism and are relatively simple to operate.

There are many variations of the **"oscillating hook" mechanism (B)**. The Class 15 and Class 66 are the most popular. Foreign manufacturers prefer the Class 15. "Class" refers to the type of shuttle used.

The third type of shuttle system is the **"rotary" shuttle (C)**. The rotary mechanism makes a complete revolution instead of back and forth like the oscillating type.

Figure 113 Shuttle Assembly

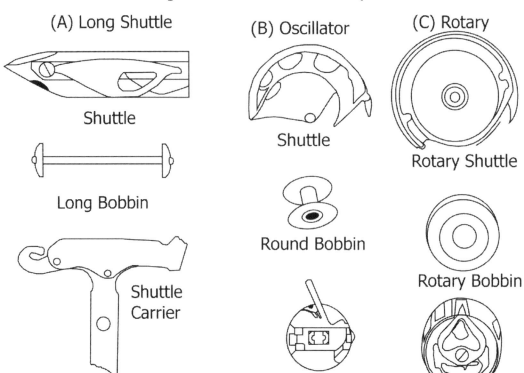

(A) Long Shuttle

Shuttle

Long Bobbin

Shuttle
Carrier

(B) Oscillator

Shuttle

Round Bobbin

Bobbin Case

(C) Rotary

Rotary Shuttle

Rotary Bobbin

Bobbin Case

12 TIMING NEEDLE BAR TO SHUTTLE - CLASS 15

The needle bar on the conventional Class 15 machine is controlled by a connecting link, fixed to a stud that is threaded into the main shaft cam. Figure 114 shows the relation of the cam to the needle bar, and the parts that must be removed to disassemble it. Screw 114A is accessible through a hole cut in the body under the machine arm. To loosen screw 114A, turn it counter clockwise allowing the needle bar to be removed, or timed, whichever is necessary. The Class 15 Sewing machine can be timed at the needle bar with a simple adjustment.

Turn the hand wheel until the take-up arm is at its highest point of travel. Move the hand wheel toward the front of the machine until the set screw (114A) is visible through the access hole.

Remove both screws, then remove the needle plate. Loosen the set screw (114A). Lower the needle bar manually while turning the hand wheel to the front of the machine until the shuttle point aligns with the needle eye.

As the shuttle point comes close to the needle eye, set the shuttle point about 3/32" above the eye of the needle (Figure 115).

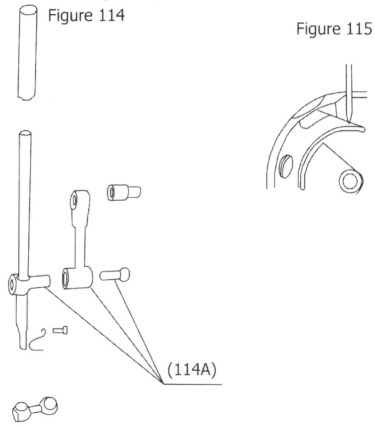

Figure 114

Figure 115

(114A)

Tighten the set screw (114A), replace the needle plate, tighten both screws, and sew a few inches on test material.

When you reset the timing on a sewing machine, always replace the needle first before doing the test sewing. The new needle will assure that you won't have a problem with a slightly bent needle or one that is otherwise damaged.

When a sewing machine is properly timed, the shuttle point will reach its intersect point just above the eye of the needle, immediately after the needle reaches its lowest point, hesitates, and starts its upward stroke.

Most late model Class 15 machines have a "timing mark" on the needle bar. To time a machine with a timing mark, remove the face plate, turn the hand wheel to the front until the set screw (114A) is visible through the access hole on the underside of the arm.

Loosen the screw and move the needle bar until the timing mark is flush with the lower end of the needle bar bushing. Tighten the set screw and replace the face plate.

CAUTION: When adjusting the needle bar, always hold the needle bar in its place so it won't twist to one side. The smallest tunl will cause the machine to skip stitches.

If this timing process seems too difficult, please have your local sewing machine repair technician complete this task.

NOTE: Before timing your machine, check the needle clamp and stop screw. Sometimes the stop screw will break off and when the needle is inserted in the clamp the needle will slide up too far, causing the machine to skip stitches or will not pick up the lower thread at all.

The Automatic Zig Zag machine got its start in the early 1950's. Elna was the first, then Pfaff, Necchi and Viking.

We will cover a Pfaff model (230/360) just to show how to time the zig zag machine.

Set the machine for the widest zig-zag stitch and put the needle position lever in the center position. Remove the face and needle plates. Turn the hand wheel until the needle is on its "down" stroke. Loosen screw "A" (Figure 116) through the opening in the needle bar frame. Hold the needle bar firmly so the needle bar does not turn. Adjust the needle to the correct height - the point of the shuttle hook should be .02" above the top of the needle eye. Position the needle bar and tighten the set screw (A).

Figure 116

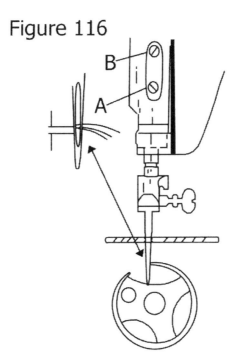

NOTE: Most sewing machines are timed generally the same - adjust the needle bar with the needle in place to the point of the shuttle that catches the upper thread and pulls the upper thread down and around the shuttle, which then picks up the lower thread, giving you the lock stitch effect.

It would be impossible to cover each of the hundreds of different models that the various manufacturers throughout the world make. However, if you understand the above procedures in general, then all you need to do to time any sewing machine is locate the screw that holds the needle bar secure, then loosen it and adjust the needle bar so the shuttle point picks up the upper thread from the needle eye as it starts its upward movement. You may have to adjust the needle bar on a trial and error basis to get your type of machine timed properly, but in many cases sewing machine service technicians must also use this trial and error method.

13 SEWING MACHINE TENSIONS

TENSION ASSEMBLY Example I - Thread Tension Unit

As a general rule most tension assemblies are nearly the same. The most important task when removing your tension unit from the machine is to MAKE SURE you lay out each part as you remove it from the shaft! In other words, make sure you know how it comes apart so that you can reassemble it in the same order as it came apart. If you place one part in the wrong position your tension will not work properly when you reinstall it in the machine! *(Tip - take pictures with your phone, if available, that you can refer back to when reassembling.)*

In the NOTES section of this book write down all of the data pertaining to your machine. For example, write down how the tension assembly came apart noting each piece as it comes off the machine. If somehow your tension parts get mixed up, or if you have to stop in the middle of the job and someone happens to come by and get the parts out of order, without the detailed notes on disassembling the tension, it would be impossible to get it back together right Figure 117 is an example of a thread tension unit, as it comes off the machine.

Figure 117

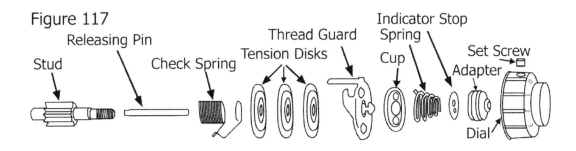

REMOVAL AND DISASSEMBLY

Open the face plate, loosen the stud screw and remove the entire tension assembly as illustrated in Figure 117. Loosen the set screw in the dial and remove the dial. Turn the adaptor to the left until it is free from the stud. Remove the indicator stop, spring, cup, and tension releasing pin. The check spring, tension discs, and thread guard should be removed from the stud as a unit (Figure 118).

Figure 118

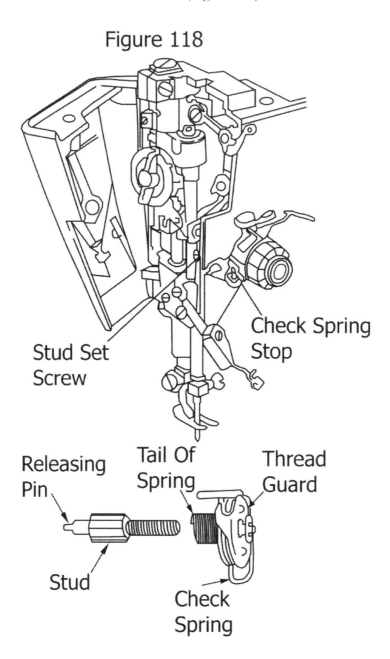

Stud Set Screw

Check Spring Stop

Releasing Pin

Tail Of Spring

Thread Guard

Stud

Check Spring

REASSEMBLY AND REPLACEMENT OF TENSION

Replace the releasing pin in the stud. Place tension discs on the thread guard, aligning the coil of the check spring with the holes in the tension discs and thread guard and place the assembly on the stud with the tail of the check spring entering the top groove of the sprocket on the stud. Replace cup spring, indicator stop and adaptor. Replace dial, making sure that the stop on the inside of the dial is in contact with the left side of the indicator stop tab when the dial is set at zero "0" tension. Tighten the set screw and insert the entire assembly into the machine, making sure the check spring is resting on the top surface of the check spring stop (Figure 118).

TENSION ASSEMBLY Example II – Graduated Tension

1. Loosen the set screw (Figure 119 "A") and remove the tension assembly from the machine.

Figure 119

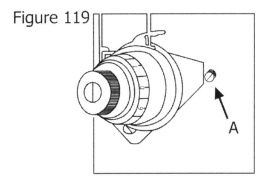

2. Turn the tension adjusting nut (Figure 120 "B") until zero on the tension index flange (Figure 120 "D") is opposite the pointer on the tension indicator (Figure 120 "G").

Figure 120

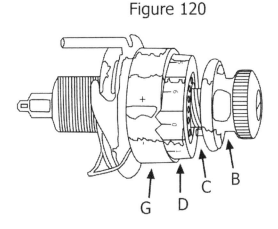

3. Next press in the index flange (Figure 120 "D") to disengage the pin (Figure 120 "C") in the tension adjusting nut (Figure 120 "B") from the flange, and remove the tension adjusting nut and flange, the flange stop, motion washer (Figure 121 "E"), tension spring (Figure 121 "F"), indicator (Figure 121 "G"), tension releasing pin (Figure 121 "J") and the tension disc assembly (Figure 121 "H") which includes the thread take-up spring, thread take-up spring thread guard and two discs.

Figure 121

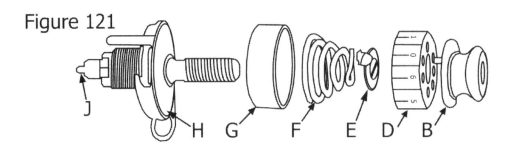

NOTE: *Always layout the parts as you remove them, in the order that they come off the stud to make for easier reassembly.*

REASSEMBLE THE TENSION UNIT

1. Put the two tension discs (Figure 122 "L") with the convex sides facing each other. Place in position on the thread take-up spring thread guard (Figure 122 "M"). Pass the eye of the thread take-up spring (Figure 122 "N") under the thread guard (Figure 122 "M"), making sure that the coils of the spring are above the tension discs.

Figure 122

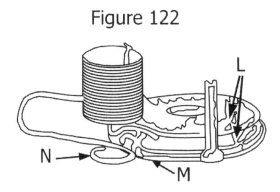

2. Put the threaded end of the tension stud (Figure 123 "0") through the coils of the take-up spring (Figure 123 "P") then through the holes in the two tension discs (Figure 123 "L") and thread guard (Figure 123 "M") and through the eye of the take-up spring, letting the end of the take-up spring enter one of the grooves in the stud (Figure 123 IIQ").

3. Next place the tension releasing pin (Figure 123 "J") in the tension stud.

Figure 123

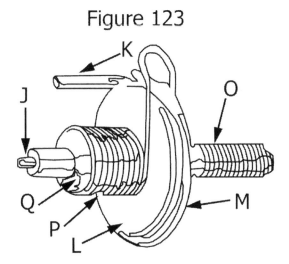

4. Hold the parts already assembled against the shoulder of the stud and put the tension indicator (Figure 124 "G") on the stud. Now insert the tension spring (Figure 124 "F") in the indicator with the first half-turn of the spring below the stud or away from the pointer of the indicator (Figure 124).

Figure 124

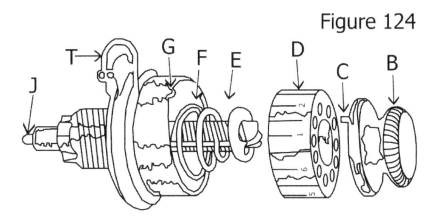

5. Now put the index flange stop washer (Figure 124 "E") on the stud with its extension toward the indicator pointer. If the spring and stop washer are in the correct position, the extension (Figure 125 "S") will clear the first coil of the spring.

Figure 125

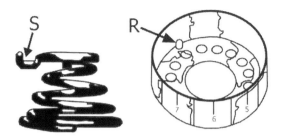

6. Put the tension index flange (Figure 124 "D") on the stud, placing it so the number 1 is opposite the pointer on the tension indicator (Figure 124 "G"), pressing it inward until the tension adjusting nut (Figure 124 "B ") can be turned onto the stud.

7. Now insert the pin (Figure 124 "E") into different holes in the flange until you find one which permits the full range of tension from light tension to tight tension to be produced with one revolution of the tension adjusting nut.

8. Lower the presser bar to eliminate the pressure on the tension releasing pin (Figure 124 "J").

9. Put the complete tension assembly back into the machine, having the long lug (Figure 123 "K ") enter the hole (Figure 126 "U"), with the pointer (Figure 124 "G") at the top, and the thread take-up spring resting on the slack thread regulator (Figure 126 "V").

Figure 126

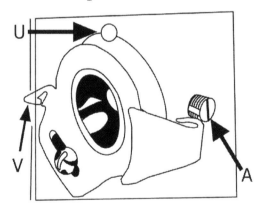

10. Push the complete tension unit in as far as it will go, then tighten the set screw (Figure 126 "A").

11. The tension of the thread take-up spring (Figure 124 "T") should be just taut enough to take up the slack of the needle thread as the eye of the needle penetrates the fabric in its downward motion. A slight adjustment in the tension on the take-up spring may be made by loosening the tension set screw (Figure 124 "A") and turning

the tension stud, with the indicator (Figure 124 "G") to the left for more tension, or to the right for less tension.

If the correct tension cannot be obtained without turning the indicator pointer (Figure 124 "G") to a position that you cannot read, remove the assembly from the machine then remove the end of the thread take-up spring from the groove (Figure 123 "Q") in the tension stud. Turn the spring and place its end in the groove in which it produces the correct tension.

The tension on the needle thread is obtained by turning the tension adjusting nut (Figure 124 "B"). If the right tension cannot be obtained by this method, adjust the tension as follows:

A) Press in the tension index flange (Figure 124 "D") to disengage the pin (Figure 124 "C") in the tension adjusting nut (Figure 124 "B") from the flange.

B) Reset the pin in one of the other holes in the flange.

C) Turn the tension adjusting nut clockwise to increase the tension.

D) Turn the tension adjusting nut counter-clockwise to decrease the tension.

TENSION ASSEMBLY Example III

The tension assembly works for two different tension jobs:

1. Pre-tension of approximately 10 grams for rewinding your bobbins, and

2. Your sewing tension adjusts from "0" to approximately 500 grams, so that you can manually adjust, with your tension dial setting, from "0" -"9".

Before you make any adjustments to your tension unit, be sure the pressure on the pull-pin in the tension assembly is released when the tension dial is set at "0" or when the presser bar is in the up or raised position.

When your presser bar is in the raised position or your tension dial is set at "0", the pre-tension applies approximately 10 grams of drag on the needle thread. When you wind a bobbin and the thread is very loosely wound and loops of thread show around the bobbin, it is an indication that your pre-tension adjustment is not correct. Too much pre-tension can and will cause your thread to break when winding a bobbin.

14 ADJUSTMENTS TO THE TENSION ASSEMBLY

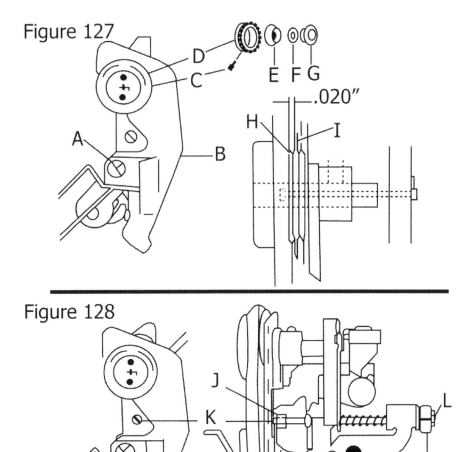

1. Remove face plate and the top cover.
2. Remove the thread guard screw "A"; swing out and remove thread guard "B".
3. Remove set screw "C".
4. Remove outer nut "D".
5. Remove inner nut "E".

NOTE: Be very careful when removing the inner nut "E". If you do not have a reversible pliers set, you can use the handle end of a small screw driver that has a rubber covering on the handle. Be sure that you do not use a metal tool on the inner nut as you may damage it.

6. Remove the slotted friction washer "F".

7. Adjust the pre-tension adjusting nut "G" clockwise to increase the drag and counter clockwise to decrease the drag on your tension.

8. Check the tension by pulling thread through the tension discs for a slight drag.

9. Replace the slotted friction washer "F" and inner nut "E".

10. Thread the outer nut "D" and check for distance between the center disc "I" and the left tension disc "H". This clearance should be approximately .020 inches.

11. Reinstall hex socket set screw "C" in the outer nut "D".

NOTE: If you still have problems with your tension adjustments after performing these steps, contact your local service technician for more in-depth repairs.

15 CLEANING, OILING AND LUBRICATION

I cannot stress enough the importance of keeping your sewing machine clean, oiled and lubricated. If you have a problem with your thread breaking or loose thread (looping up under your fabric) or stitches that are too tight, the very first step to take is to clean all lint, broken thread and dust from the machine.

CLEANING

1. Clean the lint and broken strands of thread from between the tension discs (Figure 129).

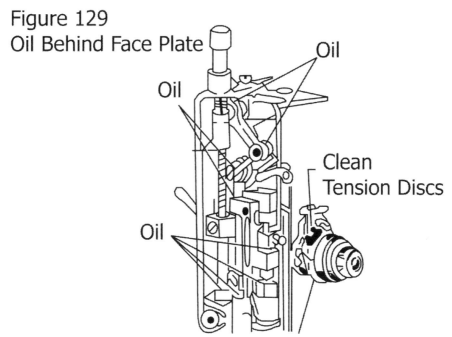

Figure 129
Oil Behind Face Plate

2. Clean the lint and broken strands of thread from around the feed dog area (Figure 130).

Figure 130

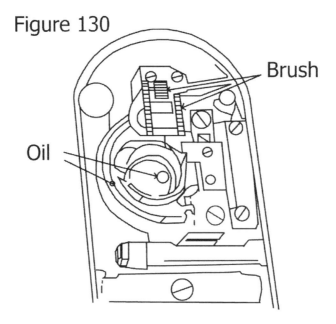

3. Clean the lint and broken pieces of thread from around the shuttle and bobbin area (Figure 130). All of the problem areas listed above can and will cause tension changes that directly affect your thread running smoothly through these areas.

OILING AND GREASING THE MACHINE

A general rule of thumb to remember is "if it moves, oil it", but keep in mind that only a drop will do! Do not over oil your sewing machine - just oil it a little more often instead.

1. Remove the two screws holding the top cover down, exposing the moving parts. Put a drop of oil on each area that moves (Figure 131).

Figure 131

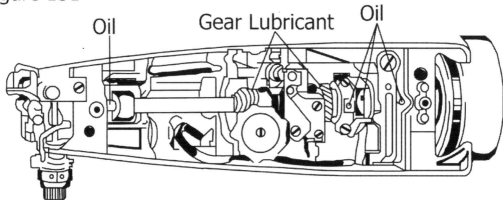

2. Grease all the gears with a light weight grease, and again, only a small amount will suffice (Figure 131). Lift the machine up to expose the bottom of the machine. All sewing machines are generally built the same. Some parts are in different places and were designed a little differently by the various manufacturers, but overall the same principles apply to all of them.

3. As you did for the top part of the machine, turn the hand wheel to note all the moving parts on the underneath part of the machine. Where two parts are joined together, there will be a bushing joining them together. Sometimes there will be a small hole where you can apply a drop of oil. If there is not a small hole, just oil the joint (Figure 132). Remember never oil the motors or belts!

Figure 132

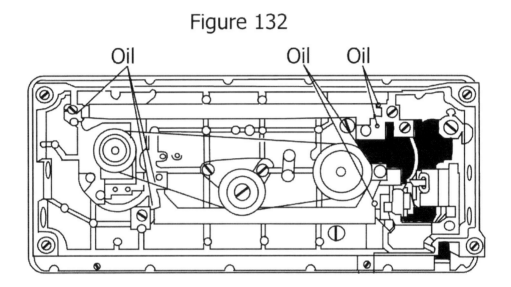

It is a good idea to make a cleaning and oiling schedule for your sewing machine, just like mechanics do for oil changes and tune ups for automobiles. Depending on the amount of sewing you do, you should mark on your calendar to do the regular cleaning and oiling every 3 months or every 6 months. This regular maintenance schedule will keep your machine running smoothly, in addition to keeping it out of the repair shop!

16 SEWING MACHINE TIMING

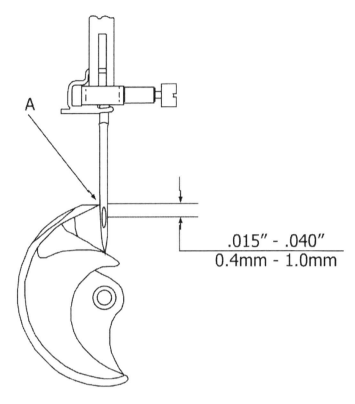

A

.015" - .040"
0.4mm - 1.0mm

GENERAL NOTE: Almost all machines are timed using the shuttle hook point and the needle (see figure above, item A). All measurements are approximate. Make sure your sewing machine shuttle hook point enters the loop made by the upper thread during the straight stitching mode and also during the widest zigzag mode. If, during any of the above stitching modes, the hook doesn't enter the thread loop made by the upper thread, then you may have to change the distance between the needle eye and where the hook point centers the needle (up or down). Example, the distance may have to be adjusted to 0.6 or 0.8 mm, according to how the manufacturer engineered the machine. This timing fact applies regardless of whether your machine has a vertical or horizontal shuttle hook system.

TIMING THE SHUTTLE HOOK TO THE NEEDLE BAR

Each manufacturer has engineered their sewing machines differently according to their particular standards. Therefore the adjustment and methods of timing the needle bar (needle) to the shuttle hook will be different, depending on whether your machine has gears, belts or other methods of adjustment. We will try to explain in detail each of the different methods used. If your machine configuration doesn't fit any of the following examples, study the examples carefully, and using your sewing and mechanical ability, you'll be able to figure out which is closest to yours.

Keep in mind - as the needle starts the UPWARD movement from the LOWEST point of its stroke, the needle thread forms a loop (see Figure P-l). It is at this time that the shuttle hook point has to enter the loop, which takes it around the bobbin case, forming the lock stitch of the lower and upper threads.

(P-1)

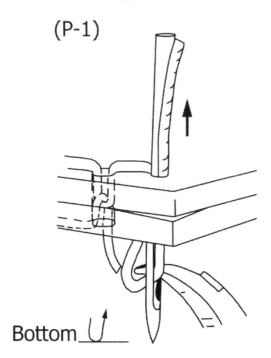

Bottom

EXAMPLE ONE: P-260/P-360 MACHINES

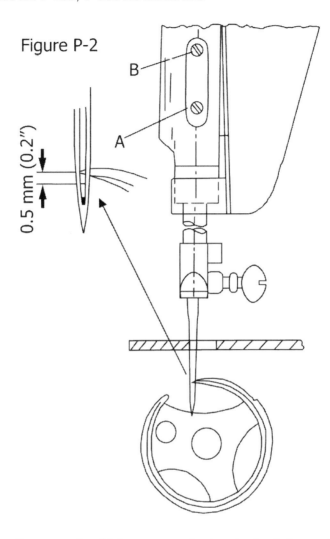

Figure P-2

To adjust, the first step should be to turn the hand wheel forward (counter clockwise) towards you until the shuttle hook is at the center of the needle (Figure P-2) and the needle MUST be on its upward movement. If the needle doesn't come all the way down to the shuttle hook and starts its upward movement before the shuttle hook gets to its top dead center point, you may have pushed the needle bar up during a sewing project by hitting a button, zipper, or some other obstruction, thereby knocking your machine out of time. This is the easiest type of timing to correct.

Loosen either one or two set screws, that secure your needle bar, while HOLDING your needle bar in its present position (axis). Let your needle bar down to a point where the shuttle hook is approximately .02/.05 mm or 3/32" above the eye of the needle. By HAND turn your machine in the forward motion (after threading the machine) just to assure the shuttle hook picks up the thread and takes it around the shuttle case. Finally, tighten the set screws securely so this will not happen again.

TIMING THE SHUTTLE HOOK TO THE NEEDLE

Some models can only be timed by adjusting the lower driving belt sprocket on its shaft (see Figures P-3 & P-4).

Figure P-3

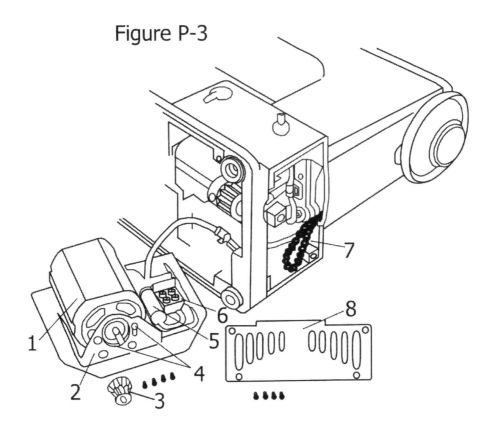

Figure P-4

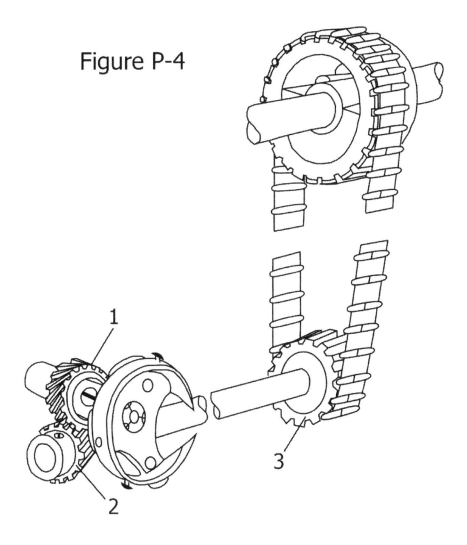

Remove side panel on hand wheel side. Two set screws on the lower drive belt gear can be reached from this position. You may have to remove the switch box to get a clear shot at the drive belt gear. After gaining access to the gear, loosen the two screws on the drive belt gear. NOTE: Make sure the needle is on its upward movement (no more than 2.0 mm on its upward stroke). Turn the shuttle hook until the point of the hook has reached the center of the needle (see Figure P-2). At this time make sure the needle and shuttle do not move - tighten the two set screws securely.

ADJUSTING NEEDLE TO THE SHUTTLE HOOK

EXAMPLE TWO/A: NECCHI STRAIGHT STITCH MACHINES

(A) Rotate hand wheel toward you (by hand) as if you were sewing (NOTE: make sure your machine is unplugged from the electrical outlet), and center the shuttle hook behind the needle (see Figure N-1).

Figure N-1

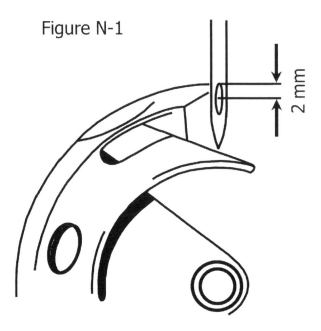

2 mm

The point of the shuttle hook should be approximately 2mm or 3/32" above the eye of the needle. To adjust the needle bar up or down to insure the correct distance above the eye of the needle (Figure N-2) loosen the set screw that holds the needle bar secure and adjust the needle bar to the above measurements. NOTE: Make sure the needle position doesn't rotate during this procedure, because then the shuttle hook will not be able to enter the thread loop (see Figure N-3 A&B).

Figure N-2

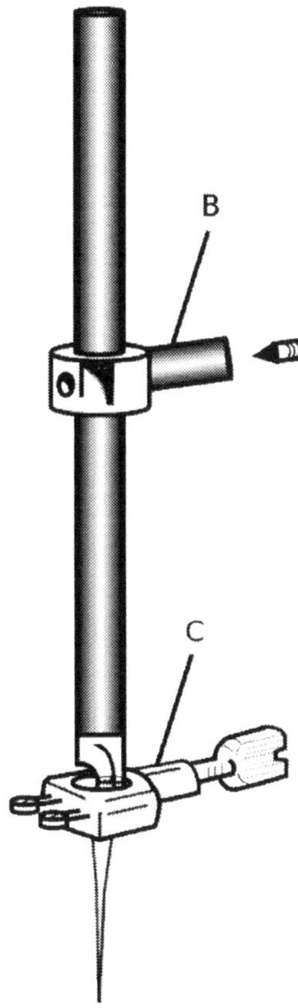

B   A

C

Figure N-3 (A & B)

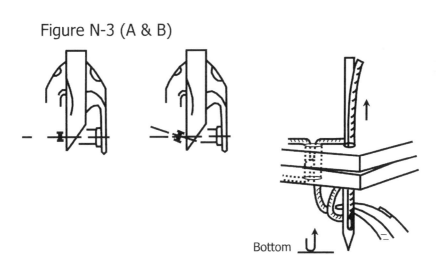

Bottom

CLEARANCE BETWEEN NEEDLE AND SHUTTLE HOOK

The needle should be as close as possible to the shuttle hook point, but the two **MUST NOT** touch each other (Figure N-4). The distance should be no more than 0.1 mm as shown.

Figure N-4

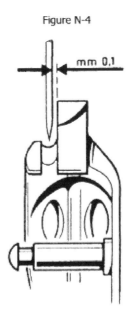

To adjust the shuttle in or out to get the desired results, loosen screw "A" (see Figure N-5) just a little, making sure the shuttle doesn't turn on its axis, then tap lightly in or out at point "B" with a brass punch.

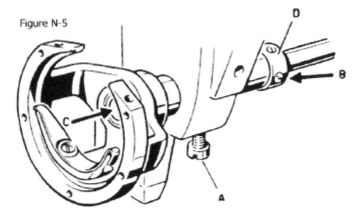

Figure N-5

NOTE: Performing this adjustment may alter the timing of your needle and shuttle hook (if shuttle rotates left or right). Check the timing adjustment (Figure N-2) and adjust if required by rotating the shuttle hook (Figure N-5). Loosen screw "A" slightly and rotate shuttle hook to obtain the desired results (Figure N-2).

SHUTTLE HOOK IN SHUTTLE CARRIER ADJUSTMENT

Figure N-6

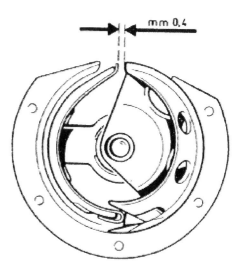

If you're having problems with your thread breaking or hanging up in the bobbin area and you've checked all other areas, you may have to make an adjustment within the shuttle 'hook/shuttle carrier mechanism.

The shuttle area is one of the most important areas of your machine. This area MUST be free of lint and dirt. All surfaces must be perfectly smooth. any rust, nicks, rough spots, etc., MUST be removed with a jewelers file and/or emery cloth.

The shuttle hook (opposite end of the hook POINT) and the shuttle carrier spring must measure 0.4 mm (1/32")(Figure N-6). If this space is larger than these measurements you will have an excess of noisy clattering. If the space is too small, your thread will hang up and break or jam around the bobbin case. This distance is factored in at the factory and cannot be adjusted except by lightly bending the shuttle carrier (spring tip area), using a brass punch and tapping lightly with a hammer. **NOTE:** This should be done by an experienced technician.

17 PRESSER BAR AND FEED DOG

THE PRESSER BAR AND ITS PURPOSE

The main purpose of the presser bar is to apply different amounts of pressure on fabric from heavy material to lightweight material. If you are having problems maintaining a good straight uniform stitch, it could be the amount of pressure that is being applied by your presser bar. In general, the heavier the material the more pressure you will need to let the feed dog walk your fabric through smoothly. The thinner or lighter the material, the less pressure you need. If the pressure is too much and you are using light weight and/or silky type material, it could cause the feed dog to damage your material and/or cause your stitches not to be uniform.

To adjust the pressure on the presser bar, and in turn, the foot, locate the thumb screw at the top of the machine (Figure N-7).

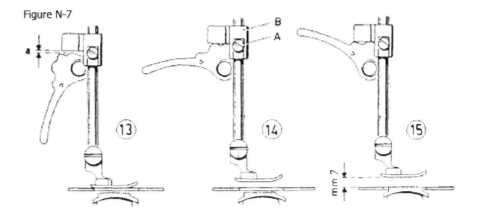

Figure N-7

By rotating the thumb screw clockwise (CW), you will increase the pressure, a counter clockwise (CCW) turn will decrease the pressure.

The correct height of the presser foot from the needle plate is 7mm (Figure N-7 #15). To adjust this clearance, loosen screw (A) and adjust the presser bar through the guide (B) (Figure N-7 #14). Secure screw (A) firmly when the correct adjustment is obtained.

The distance between the presser bar lifting arm and the presser bar guide should be 0.5mm (Figure N-7 #13). **NOTE:** Be sure the needle bar does not rotate left or right during the adjustment process. The needle must be center of the presser foot and needle plate hole. If this is not centered re-adjust to the center of both needle foot and needle plate hole.

FEED DOG ADJUSTMENTS -STRAIGHT STITCH MACHINE

The presser foot must sit flat or level with the feed dog teeth surface. If this is not the case with your machine, your fabric will not feed properly under the presser foot. Also the feed dog must have equal clearance on both sides of the feed dog and needle plate. Slowly rotate the hand wheel in a counter clockwise (CCW) direction (toward you), and check the clearance of the feed dog and needle plate slot (Figure N-8).

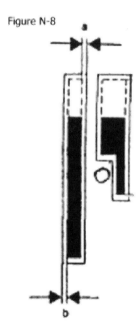

Figure N-8

Next, check to see if the feed dog and the presser foot are level with each other. Raise the foot and place a piece of thin paper on each of the four comers of the feed dog (one corner at a time). Let the foot down and see if the paper pulls out equally on each corner. If not, one of two things must be wrong. First, the presser foot may be defective and needs to be replaced. Secondly, the feed dog may be worn out and needs to be replaced.

ADJUSTING THE FEED DOG LEVEL AND EXCESSIVE CLEARANCES

Figure N-9

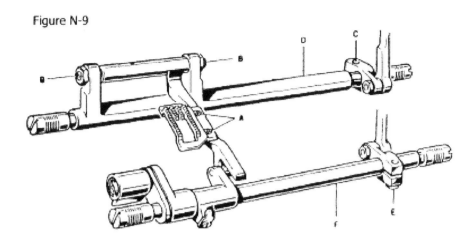

The feed dog must be parallel to the needle plate slot (Figure N-8). Most often you can make any adjustments needed by loosening two screws (Figure N-9 Item A) and adjust accordingly. After you have made the adjustments securely tighten the screws again. If this doesn't correct your clearances, then, with the stitch lever or knob set for its longest stitch (Figure N-10 Item A) the distance at the beginning travel of the feed dog above the needle plate should be 0.4 mm.

Figure N-10

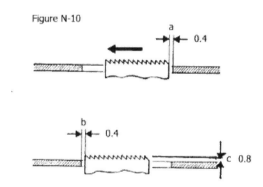

To adjust the clearance, loosen screw (C) (Figure N-9), turn the shaft (B/D) slowly to obtain the desired clearance. Securely tighten screw (C).

The feed dog teeth projection above the needle plate should be 0.8mm (Fig. N-10 Item C). Rotate the handwheel in a counter clockwise (CCW) direction until the feed dog is at its highest position. Check the distance and adjust if required. Loosen screw (E) (Figure N-9) and turn shaft (F) as necessary to obtain the proper clearance. Securely tighten screw (E).

Almost all of the instructions given on the straight stitch machine example above will generally apply to zigzag sewing machines also. The following exceptions are noted.

NEEDLE/SHUTTLE CLEARANCE - ZIGZAG

The only variation from the straight stitch sewing machine and the zigzag machine in timing the needle and shuttle is the securing screw position (Figure N-11 Item A). Go back to the beginning of example #2 and follow those instructions to adjust the needle/shuttle timing.

Figure N-11

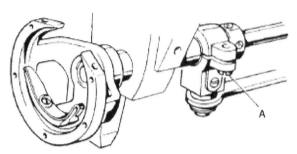

A

FREE-ARM SEWING MACHINES

Exceptions from the straight stitch machine to the free arm machines are noted in Fig. N-12.

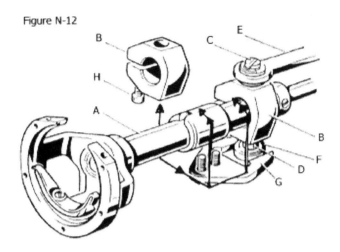

Figure N-12

A small clamp "B" is secured onto shaft "A" (Figure N-12) on the shuttle carrier. Pins "C" and "D" are secured to this small block with two screws. Pin "C" connects rod "E" which controls the axial run of the shuttle carrier when sewing in the zigzag mode. The bottom pin "D" carries roller "F" while sliding inside fork "G", will not allow the shuttle carrier to turn around its axis.

ADJUSTING NEEDLE TO SHUTTLE CLEARANCE

Loosen clamp screw "H" (Figure N-12) just enough to move as close as possible but not touching. Secure screw "H" firmly.

18 MACHINES WITH SLANTING SHUTTLE ROTARY HOOK

EXAMPLE THREE:

SHUTTLE HOOK AND NEEDLE TIMING

Place your sewing machine in the straight stitch sewing position.

Turn the hand wheel by hand counter-clockwise until the needle is at its lowest point. Gently move the hand wheel backward and forward to insure you have the bottom dead center. As the needle starts its upward movement, no more than 2.5 mm, the shuttle hook point should be in the center of the needle (Figure N-13).

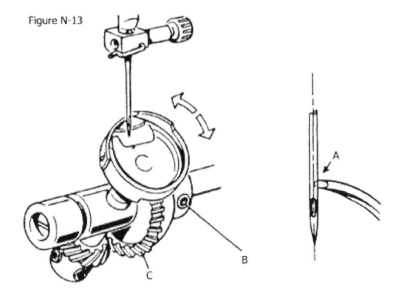

Figure N-13

The required adjustments will be as follows. Loosen screw "B" of gear "C" (be sure to keep the hand wheel motionless). Rotate the shuttle hook until the shuttle point is centered on the needle (Figure N-13, Item A). Tighten screw "B" securely.

Adjust the zigzag width control to its maximum position. Turn the handwheel counter clockwise (CCW) by hand, then place the needle position lever to the left position (L/M/R). Lower the needle to its lowest position. When the needle starts its upward movement, the shuttle point should be centered on the needle. The shuttle hook point should center the needle approximately 0.4/6 mm above the needle eye. If you need to adjust the shuttle hook point (Figure N-14), loosen screw "A" and adjust the needle bar up or down. Secure screw "A" tightly before proceeding.

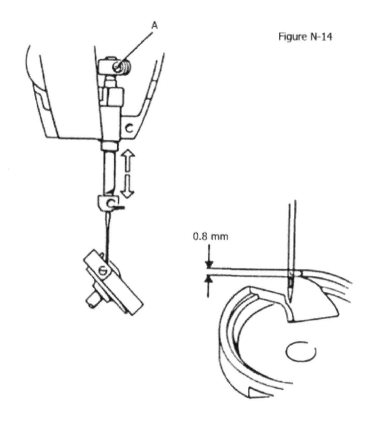

Figure N-14

Test the machine's ability to pick up thread by threading the machine and turning the handwheel by hand (CCW) to insure the shuttle hook point enters the thread loop. Now move the needle back to the middle position (L/M/R) and try sewing normally. If any further adjustments need to be made to fine tune the machine, go back to the beginning and make further adjustments as needed, following the guidelines already given.

19 MACHINES WITH GEARS

EXAMPLE FOUR:

TIMING THE SHUTTLE HOOK AND ADJUSTING THE NEEDLE BAR TO CORRECT HEIGHT.

The needle bar height should be adjusted as follows. Rotate the hand wheel (CCW) toward you until the needle is at its dead bottom position. The shuttle hook point should be centered behind the needle. The position of the needle should be around .004" from the hook point and the shuttle should be approximately 0.01mm above the needle eye (Figure S-1). **NOTE:** If the needle doesn't come all the way down to the shuttle hook point, you've probably hit a zipper, button, or a straight pin while sewing, which pushed the needle bar up, causing your machine to be knocked out of time.

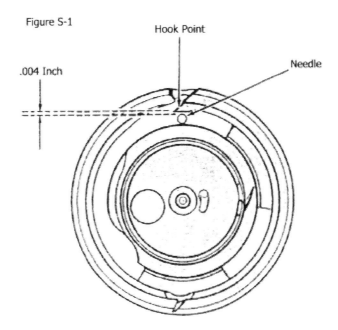

Figure S-1

Hook Point

Needle

.004 Inch

Place the machine in the straight stitch position. The upper timing mark on the needle bar will be aligned with the bottom edge of the needle bar bushing. With the needle at its BDC position, loosen the needle bar clamping screw then raise or lower the needle bar as needed. Be sure the needle bar doesn't rotate during the task. Tighten the needle bar screw tightly (Figure S-2).

Figure S-2

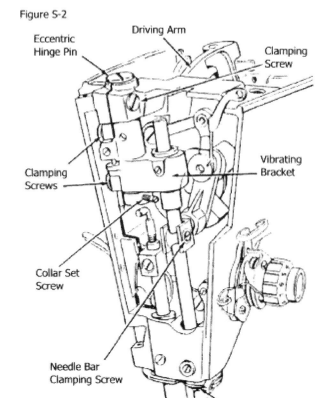

Driving Arm

Eccentric
Hinge Pin

Clamping
Screw

Clamping
Screws

Vibrating
Bracket

Collar Set
Screw

Needle Bar
Clamping Screw

Upper Timing
Mark

TIMING THE SHUTTLE HOOK

Perform the previous task first (needle height). Install a new needle, remove the throat plate, bed slide reel cover and bottom cover plate. Remove the feed dog so the point of the shuttle hook can be seen. (Do this only if you can't see the shuttle hook point).

Place the needle in the straight stitch position. Rotate the handwheel counter clockwise (CCW) toward you until the timing mark on the needle bar is at the bottom of the needle bar bushing. The needle bar should be just starting on its <u>upward movement</u>, with the needle bar at its timing mark as stated above. The shuttle hook point should be in the center of the needle (Figure S-3). **NOTE:** The distance should be approximately 0.4mm above the needle eye in order for the hook point to enter the thread loop created by the upper thread as it starts its upward movement.

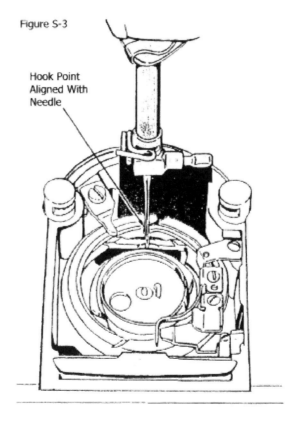

Figure S-3

Hook Point
Aligned With
Needle

If the hook doesn't center the needle, loosen the two set screws in the horizontal bevel gear (Figure S-4).

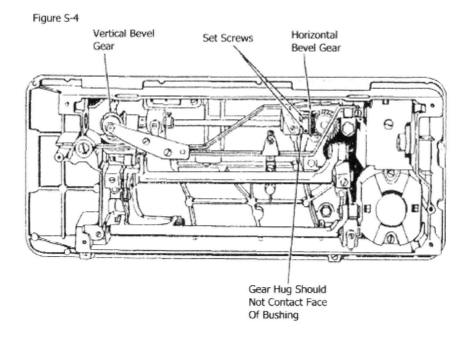

Figure S-4

Vertical Bevel Gear   Set Screws   Horizontal Bevel Gear

Gear Hug Should Not Contact Face Of Bushing

DO NOT let the needle bar move while loosening the set screws. Rotate the vertical bevel gear until the shuttle hook point is centered behind the needle. Secure tightly the two screws on the horizontal bevel gear. At this point make sure both gears are meshed correctly without binding and the gear base is not touching the bushing face.

20 MACHINES WITH BELT DRIVE ASSEMBLY

EXAMPLE FIVE:

TIMING THE SHUTTLE HOOK TO THE NEEDLE

Place the needle in the center position. Place stitch width to "0" position. Install a new needle, size 18. Rotate handwheel counter clockwise (CCW) toward you until the lower timing mark is aligned on needle bars' upward movement (Figure S-5).

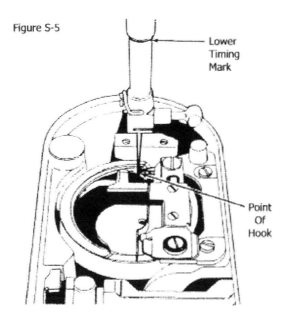

Figure S-5

Lower Timing Mark

Point Of Hook

At this point the shuttle hook point should be at the middle of the needle approximately 0.4 mm above the needle eye. Be sure the timing mark doesn't move during this task.

Figure S-6

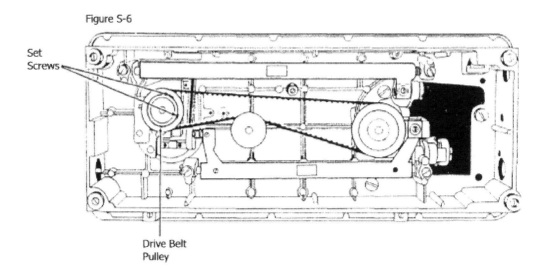

Set
Screws

Drive Belt
Pulley

Loosen the two set screws (Figure S-6). Rotate the shuttle hook point until the point of the shuttle hook is centered behind the needle. Press down on the shuttle as you tighten the two set screws tightly. Check the shuttle hook for binding. The shuttle should run smoothly with no vertical movement. Replace all parts removed while performing this task.

Test sew on a fabric scrap to see that the machine is running smoothly and properly.

TIMING SHUTTLE HOOK TO NEEDLE BELT DRIVEN MACHINES

EXAMPLE SIX:

Set the zigzag to "0" and the needle to the center position.

Turn the sewing machine on its side so the bottom of the machine is exposed. Rotate hand wheel (CCW) towards you until the three screws are visible (Figure V-1).

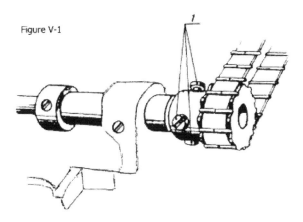

Figure V-1

Loosen each of the three screws, adjust the needle bar to its lowest point and starting on its upward movement (approximately .098"). Check the position of the needle and shuttle hook eye. Adjust the shuttle hook point until the hook is centered behind the needle (Figure V-2).

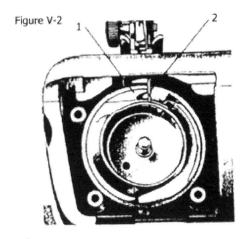

Figure V-2

CAUTION: Do not let the driver shaft move as you adjust the shuttle on the shaft. Snugly tighten one set screw and check timing by threading machine and checking to see if the hook enters the loop made by the upper thread. If this task checks out, tighten the other two screws.

TIMING THE NEEDLE BAR TO SHUTTLE HOOK

Figure V-3

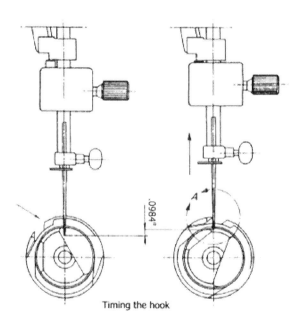

Timing the hook

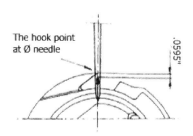

Setting the needle bar height

Set the sewing machine for straight stitch sewing. Turn the hand wheel until the needle bottoms out and starts its upward movement. The shuttle hook should be centered above the eye of the needle (approximately .059") (Figure V-3).

Loosen the needle bar set screw (the screw that secures the needle bar). Secure needle bar firmly so it doesn't rotate while you adjust up or down to obtain the proper clearance between the eye of the needle and the shuttle hook point. Tighten the set screw.

Test sew on a fabric scrap to make sure the machine is sewing smoothly.

21 "MODEL NUMBER" CHART – BRO. SERIES

The following "Model Number" chart applies to the machines throughout the next section. Compare your model number to those in the chart to see if it applies to the writings in the "Example Seven" Bro. section.

MODEL NUMBERS

GROUP A	GROUP B	GROUP C	GROUP D	GROUP E	GROUP F	GROUP G
M451	XL791	M461, 471	XL700	XL703	M875	M401, M601
	M791	M761, 771				
M751	M803	XL711	M865	M795		
		B606, 607				
B801	B803	B701, 704	B604	B703	B875	B401, B601

ADJUSTING NEEDLE BAR HEIGHT

EXAMPLE SEVEN: BRO-M-1:

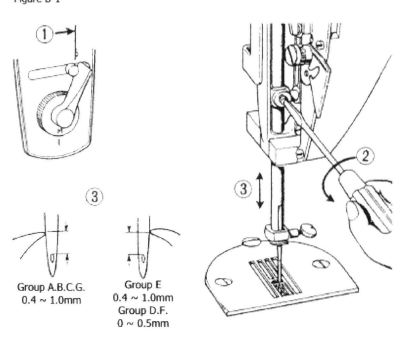

Figure B-1

Group A.B.C.G.
0.4 ~ 1.0mm

Group E
0.4 ~ 1.0mm
Group D.F.
0 ~ 0.5mm

Adjust the pattern selector knob to M (on model XL703, turn to No.1).

Set zigzag width to "5". Place the needle (L/M/R) to the RIGHT position. (Free arm machines place the needle to the LEFT side. Turn the handwheel by hand to position the needle to the left or right, depending on which type machine you have.

Loosen the set screw on the needle bar (see item 2 on Figure B-1). Adjust the needle bar up or down so the distance between the top of the needle eye and the shuttle tip is from 0.5 to 1.0mm above the needle eye (Item 3 Figure B-1).

Secure the needle bar set screw (Item 2) firmly. Rotate the handwheel toward you counter clockwise (CCW) by hand to verify that the shuttle hook tip enters the thread loop made by the upper thread when it descends into the shuttle area. Further adjustments may need to be made following the above instructions. **NOTE:** Before starting this task, install a new needle and insure the needle is all the way up in the needle clamp and seated firmly against the needle stop pin.

SHUTTLE HOOK POINT CLEARANCE - ALL TRANSVERSE RACE MODELS

Figure B-2

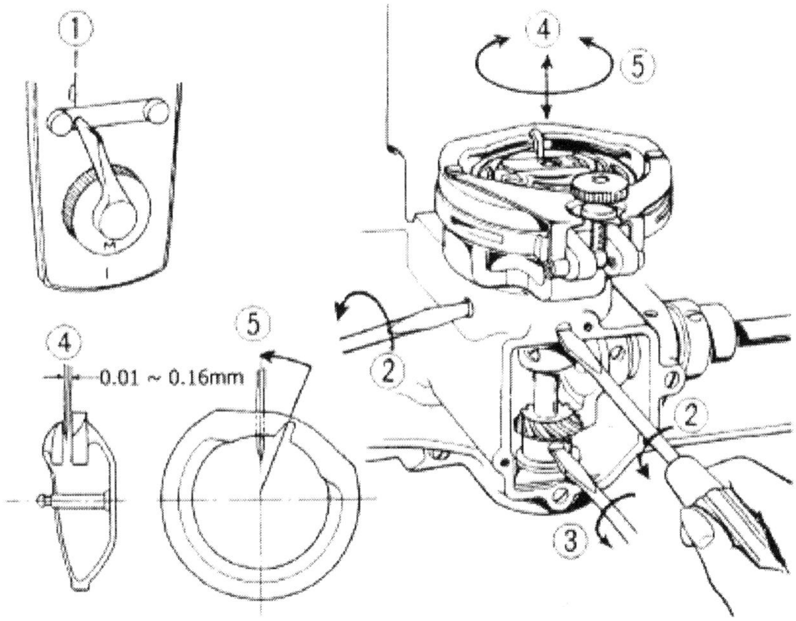

Adjust the zigzag width lever to "0" and the needle position to "M" (Item 1 Figure B-2).

Loosen the two screws holding the gear box cover exposing the race way (Item 2 Figure B-2). Slightly loosen the two screws on the shuttle drive shaft bevel gear (Item 3 Figure B-2).

Adjust the shuttle race (0.01 to 0.16mm) between the needle and shuttle hook point (Item 4 Figure B-2). Insure the needle doesn't hit the shuttle point.

Adjust the raceway so the notch of the raceway comes to the center of the needle (Item 5 Figure B-2).

TIMING SHUTTLE HOOK TO NEEDLE - ALL TRANSVERSE RACE MODELS AND FREE ARM MODELS

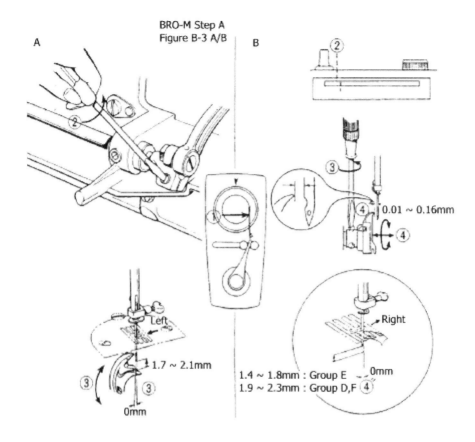

Adjust the zigzag width lever to "5" (Item 1 Figure B-3), and move the needle to the far left side of the needle slot (Item 3 Figure B-3A).

Loosen the screw in the lower shaft crank just enough to adjust (Item 2 Fig. B-3A)

Rotate the handwheel toward you (counter clockwise) and bring the needle to its lowest level. Adjust the needle bar raise so the shuttle hook point intersects with the needle when it is on its upward movement. Adjust the raise to 1.7 to 2.1 mm (Item 3 Figure B-3A). Make this adjustment by turning the handwheel counter clockwise (towards you) while holding the shuttle hook in place. Secure the set screw firmly (Item 2 Figure B-3A).

BRO-M Step B

Adjust the zigzag width to "5" (Item 1 Figure B-3A). For Model XL703, adjust pattern indicator at cam #1 and put the needle in the far right position in the needle plate slot (Item 4 Figure B-3B)

Slightly loosen the rotary hook screw (Item 3 Figure B-3B). Adjust the shuttle hook so the distance between the hook point and needle is set at 0.01 to 0.16 mm, by moving it back and forth (Item 4 Figure B-3 B).

HEIGHT OF PRESSER BAR - ALL MODELS

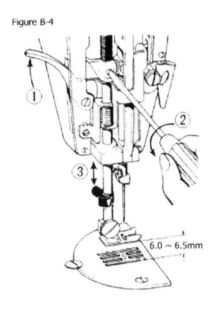

Figure B-4

Adjust the presser bar lever to the up position (Item 1, Figure B-4) Slightly loosen the presser bar set screw (Item 2 Figure B-4) just enough so you can move the bar up or down. **NOTE:** Hold the bar firmly; do not let the bar twist left or right. The foot must be parallel or in alignment with the feed dog.

Measure the distance between the bottom of the presser foot and the needle plate surface (Item 3 Figure B-4). The clearance should be 6.0 to 6.5mm. Adjust this measurement accordingly.

Secure the set screw (Item 2 Figure B-4) firmly. During this check, be sure the presser foot is installed correctly - all the way up before tightening the thumb screw that holds the presser foot in place. **CAUTION:** If your machine has a thread cutter on the presser bar, be careful that you don't slip and cut yourself during the adjustment of the needle bar.

ADJUSTMENT OF FEED CAM - ALL MODELS

Figure B-5

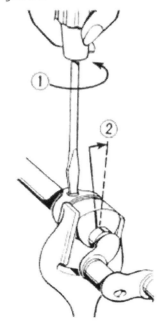

The top cover must be removed to expose the feed cam in order to loosen the set screw (Item 1 Figure B-5). Adjust the feed cam so the two marks on the feed cam and upper shaft align as per Item 2 Figure B-5. Secure the set screw firmly.

ADJUSTMENT OF THE VERTICAL FEED CAM - ALL TRANSVERSE RACE MODELS AND GROUP "D"

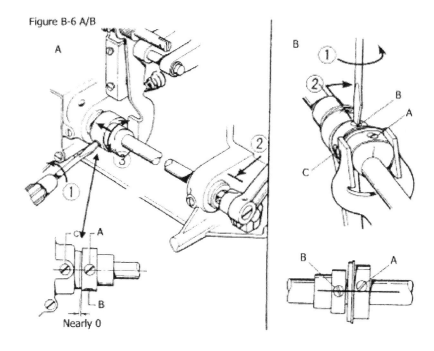

Figure B-6 A/B

Remove the bottom plate to expose the vertical feed cam, if your machine has a bottom plate. Loosen the vertical feed cam set screws (2) just enough so the cam will move (Item 1 Figure B-6A).

Rotate the handwheel toward you (counter clockwise) and bring the crank rod to its lowest level (Item 2 Figure B-6A).

Adjust the vertical feed cam so the distance between the feed cam and the shaft bushing is less than 0.3 mm - insure that screw "A" and "C" are in alignment with each other - in a straight line across from each other (Item 3 Figure B-6A). Secure set screw "B" firmly.

After you have adjusted the feed cam in Figure B-6A, loosen the two screws "B" and "C" on the vertical feed cam (Item 1 Figure B-6B). Check the alignment of the two screws ("A" and "B"). The alignment should be as indicated in the lower diagram in Figure B-6B. Secure the set screws "B" and "C" firmly.

ADJUSTING THE HEIGHT OF THE FEED DOG - ALL MODELS

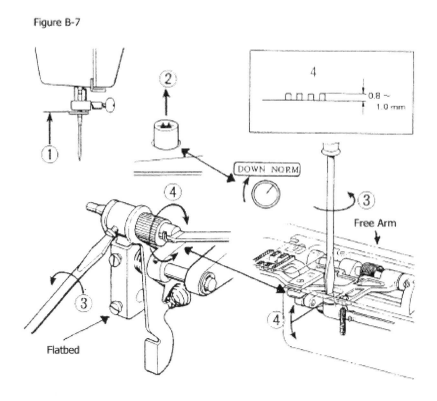

Figure B-7

Rotate the handwheel towards you (counter clockwise) and bring the needle to its highest position (Item 1 Figure B-7).

Set the feed dog to its highest level "UP" position (this is normally located at the right bottom side of the machine) (Item 2 Figure B-7).

Loosen the guide ring set screw (on free arm machines it is located on the drop feed adjusting arm). Loosen only enough to make the adjustment.

Adjust the GUIDE RING to obtain the correct distance between the needle plate and the feed dog top of teeth (0.8 to 1.0 mm). Item 4 upper right diagram.

For free-arm machines adjust the drop feed adjusting arm as indicated in Item 3 and 4 Figure B-7.

SHUTTLE DRIVER SHAFT AND RACEWAY CLEARANCE SEPARATION - ALL MODELS EXCEPT FREE-ARM

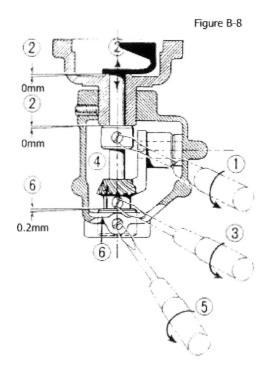

Figure B-8

Remove the gear box cover and loosen the two set screws on collar for the driver shaft (Item 1 Figure B-8). Loosen the screws just enough to make any adjustments.

The clearance should be very close, per diagram in Item 2. Set both distances at 0.0 mm.

Next, loosen the two set screws on the shuttle driver shaft BEVEL GEAR (Item 3 Figure B-8). Adjust the driver shaft gear to fit snugly, but not too tight, to the lower shaft gear (Item 4 Figure B-8).

Next loosen the set screw on the shuttle driver shaft bushing (Item 5) and adjust the bushing at 0.2 mm (Item 6), so the distance between the bushing and driver shaft gear will be correct. Insure that all set screws are tightened firmly. Now check the operation of the machine to insure there is no binding and it operates smoothly. Rotate the handwheel by hand at the beginning as you check the operation of the machine.

ZIGZAG WIDTH ADJUSTMENT - ALIGNMENT OF HOLES, MAXIMUM DISTANCE - ALL MODELS

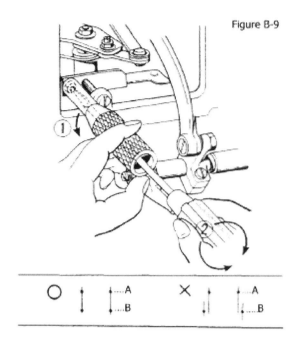

Figure B-9

(A) Set needle position "L" and "M", zigzag width "O" left and right holes.

(B) Set needle position "M", zigzag width to "5", left and right holes.

Loosen the lock nut, while holding the adjusting screw in place (Item 1 Figure B-9). **NOTE:** If you don't have a box driver wrench as indicated by the diagram, use an off-set box wrench and a screw driver to hold the adjusting screw stead while loosening the lock nut (Item 2). On free-arm machines you will need to remove the base plate.

Now you can rotate the adjusting screw to obtain the correct stitching as per example "O" in the lower left of the diagram.

ZIGZAG SATIN STITCH SEAMS ALL MODELS

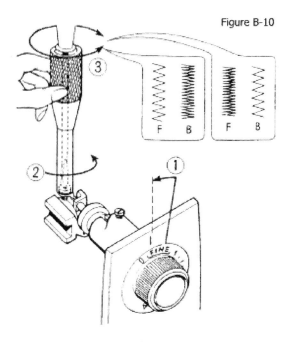

Figure B-10

Set stitch length to "Fine" and zigzag width to "5" (Item 1 Figure B-10). Use a box wrench to loosen the locknut, while holding the adjusting screw with a screw driver. Don't let the adjusting screw move during the loosening of the lock nut (Item 2 & 3 Figure B-10).

At this time adjust the screw left or right to obtain the correct satin stitching forward or backwards. Fine tune until the stitching is correct.

FEED REGULATOR GROOVED CAM ADJUSTMENT - ALL MODELS

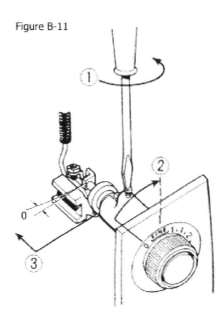

Figure B-11

Loosen the screw on bushing (Item 1 Figure B-11). Adjust the stitch length to "0" (Item 2). Rotate the grooved cam (Item 3) so a clearance of "0" is between the feed regulator adjusting plate and the direction control stud. Secure the screw (Item 1) firmly. Test sew and make any fine tuning as per above instructions.

ADJUSTMENT TO CENTER NEEDLE IN NEEDLE PLATE - ALL MODELS

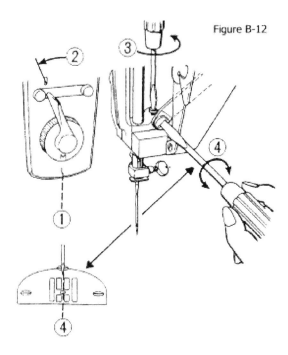

Figure B-12

Set the needle position to middle (M) (Item 1 Figure B-12). Adjust the zigzag width lever to "0" and use the straight stitch needle plate (Item 2).

Loosen the eccentric stud set screw slightly – just enough to allow movement. Now you can adjust the eccentric stud (Item 3) to set the needle to its center position in the straight stitch needle plate (Item 4). Secure the set screw (Item 3) firmly. Rotate the handwheel by hand to confirm the needle is correctly centered. **NOTE:** Before starting this task, always install a new needle and check to verify that the needle is not bent.

22 TROUBLE SHOOTING CHART FOR EXAMPLE SEVEN MACHINES:

Various problems will be listed with possible reasons for each problem, as well as instructions regarding which of the procedures detailed earlier in this section should be used to solve the problems.

IMPROPER TIMING OF NEEDLE AND SHUTTLE HOOK

See Figures B -1 & 2 and detailed instructions for correction.

MATERIAL NOT FEEDING

A. Improper positioning of needle plate – see instruction book "to change needle plate" section for all models.

B. Not enough pressure on presser foot – see FigureB-4 and previously discussed instructions for correction.

C. Improper setting of feed cam – see Figure B-5

D. Improper positioning of vertical feed cam – see Figure B-6 and detailed instructions.

E. Improper height of feed dog - See Figure B-7.

NEEDLE KEEPS BREAKING

A. Incorrect needle position - See instruction book "to change the needle" section for all models.

B. Wrong clearance between needle and shuttle hook – See Figure B-2 and B-3 A&B for correcting problem.

SLOW RUNNING MACHINE

A. *Machine dry of oil* - See instruction book "Oiling your machine" section - all models.

B. *Lint and thread build-up in shuttle and feed dog area* – See instruction book "Cleaning the shuttle hook area and your feed dog area" section - all models.

NOISY MACHINE

A. *Machine dry of oil* – Oil the machine per your instruction book - all models.

B. *Shuttle shaft not set right* – See Figure B-8 for instructions on how to correct problem.

ZIGZAG WIDTH TOO WIDE

A. *Zigzag width setting is adjusted improperly* – See Figure B-9 for instructions on how to correct the problem.

SEAMS UNEVEN

A. *Grooved cam feed regulator not set properly* - See Figure B-10 for instructions to correct the problem.

B. *Feed regulator not set properly* – See Figure B-11.

NEEDLE ALIGNMENT WITH NEEDLE SLOT NOT SET RIGHT

1. *Needle not centered* – See Figure B-12 for instructions to correct the problem.

LOWER THREAD BREAKS

A. *Bobbin has a nick or is bent* – Change bobbins.

B. *Bobbin spring has a nick or is scratched where thread pulls through* - Change the bobbin case, or replace the spring where the thread pulls under.

C. *Bobbin case tension too tight* - Adjust screw counter clockwise to relieve pressure on thread. See instruction book under "adjusting lower tension" section.

D. *Shuttle hook point area has a nick or rough spot* – Change out shuttle hook unit or remove scratch or nick.

UPPER THREAD BREAKS

A. *Nick or scratch on shuttle hook* - Change shuttle or remove nick.

B. *Upper thread tension too tight* - Adjust tension to lower number and check to see if some thread has broken off between the tension discs.

C. *Needle size too small for thread or needle eye has a sharp edge* - Change needle to new size.

D. *Needle bent or has a blunt point* - Change to a new needle.

E. *Machine has been threaded wrong* - Check your manual for proper threading procedure.

F. *Needle plate incorrect or damaged at point where needle goes through the hole* - Change needle plate.

23 WHEN YOUR CHILD WANTS TO SEW

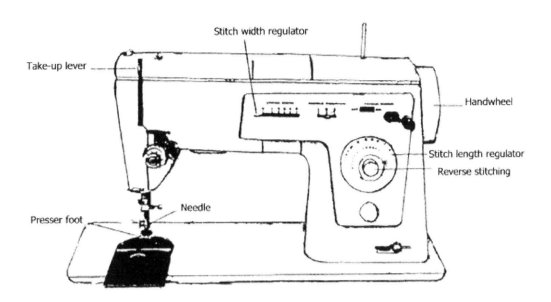

There may come a time when your children or grandchildren will want to learn how to sew. Very small children should learn the basics of sewing first via the hand sewing method - using sewing cards, then graduating up to hand sewing doll clothes, small pillows, and sewing on large buttons, using a very large needle, loose woven fabric and heavy thread.

As the child matures he or she will want to learn to use the sewing machine as well. You know the maturity level of your child better than anyone, so if the child shows an interest in learning to use the machine, then you can determine if they will be able to learn and follow the necessary sewing rules and steps to using a sewing machine.

To begin with, simply show the child the basics of sewing machine operation and where the sewing machine parts are that he or she will be using (see Figure 133 above). Start simply with straight stitching, then some zigzag stitching, starting and stopping the sewing machine, removing the fabric from the needle area, and keeping their fingers out from under the needle. Don't confuse your child by trying to show them how to take a needle out, or how to re-wind a bobbin, or the like until after they've had considerable experience with the basic sewing techniques (you do the bobbin changing, needle changing, etc.), and are ready to learn some new things.

Sewing machine care and maintenance will change a little after children start to use the machine. The following recommendations will make life a little easier for you if your child was the last one to use the machine.

1. Always wipe the machine down with a damp cloth - sometimes children may have sticky fingers, and you don't want to start out with spots on your fabric before the garment is even finished!

2. Always check the stitch length and width – you may be used to leaving it on a certain setting, which could have easily been changed while the child was sewing.

3. Clean the lint from the tension discs, throat plate area, and bobbin area at least monthly. Nothing will cause more problems than a build-up of lint and broken thread pieces.

4. Make a new cleaning and oiling schedule for the machine, especially if you do a lot of sewing, and now your son or daughter is also doing a lot of sewing.

5. Take out the needle and roll it on the sewing table to be certain it is not bent. Check the point on the needle to see that it isn't rough. If there's any question whether the needle is still good or not, replace it.

6. Check the size of the needle - - your child may have been hemming a pair of jeans with a large heavy duty needle. Check for compatibility; don't risk damaging a new silk blouse!

24 HINTS FOR THE SEWER/CRAFTER

1. Always turn the hand wheel of your sewing machine toward you, never turn it away from you once the machine has been threaded. Also never run a threaded sewing machine unless there is a piece of fabric under the presser foot, this is probably the easiest way to jam the machine, break needles and throw the machine out of timing! To eliminate the possibility of a child doing damage to your machine, always unplug it after finishing for the day.

2. Before beginning to sew, lay both threads under and toward the back of the presser foot. The correct way of bringing the bobbin thread up after changing the bobbin is as follows (figure 134):

Figure 134

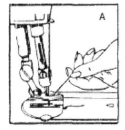 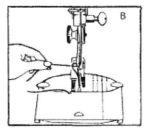 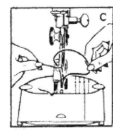 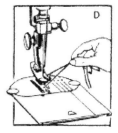

A) While holding the top thread with the left hand, turn the handwheel with the right hand until the needle is all the way down into the bobbin area.

B) Keep holding the thread and rotating the handwheel, bring the needle up to the highest point. As the needle comes up, a loop of bobbin thread will come up with it. Pull on the top thread to draw up more of the bobbin thread.

C) Turn loose of the top thread, and pull on the loop of the bobbin thread to bring up the free end of the bobbin thread.

D) Pass both the top and bobbin threads under the presser foot and take them back toward the right. Both thread ends should be at least 4" long to prevent them from being pulled into the bobbin and jamming as you begin sewing.

3. When beginning or ending a seam, make sure the take-up lever is in its highest position.

4. Put a drop of oil into the hook/shuttle area regularly.

5. About once every six months spray all moving parts with a rust preventative fluid (like WD-40). This is done to prevent the buildup of a light trace of rust on the metal surfaces. (**CAUTION:** Do not spray directly into the motor.)

6. Be sure that the needle is in the center position when straight stitching. Never straight stitch with the needle in the left or right positions (an exception to this is when using a zipper foot).

7. It will save a great deal of "total working time" on a project if you will take care of the thread ends as each bit of stitching is completed. If you fail to do this, it will take extra time when the project is finished to trace out each loose hanging piece of thread in order to clip it. If you just leave the loose pieces of thread hanging, it will detract from the overall professional look of the garment.

8. In some types of fabric, such as chiffon, you may find the needle will drag the fabric down into the needle hole when you begin to sew. Make sure you are using a fine needle, have the tensions set properly, and if the problem still exists, place a piece of gummed tape over the needle hole in the throat plate of the machine. The tape will prevent the fabric from being "pulled" down, and can be removed easily later.

9. Back-stitching at the end of a line of machine stitching firmly fastens the end, but sometimes can cause puckering of the fabric. To prevent this, hold the fabric taut as you continue to operate the machine, taking several stitches in the same spot in the fabric. These several stitches will secure the thread, but use your own judgment in using this method, as you could cause damage to very fine lightweight fabrics.

10. Hinged presser feet on sewing machines require different handling from rigid ones because the pressure of the foot is less evenly distributed throughout its entire length. The threads have a tendency to tangle at the beginning of the stitching and the machine may stall on the tangled threads. Hold the loose thread ends gently with the right hand as you begin stitching. If the threads are slightly taut, they cannot tangle or be pulled down into the bobbin area to cause a jam.

11. To protect your sewing machine while it is not in use, you should place a piece of fabric under the presser foot and lower the foot onto it. Also, be sure to cover the machine, as any dust settling in and around the moving parts can cause sewing problems later on.

12. Never oil your sewing machine without first cleaning it as well as you can, removing all the dust, lint, and pieces of thread from the bobbin area and throat plate area.

13. There are three main points to be aware of each time the sewing machine is used: 1) Make sure the take-up lever is at its highest point when stitching is started and when the work is being removed from the machine. 2) Always drop the presser foot before changing the tension on the upper thread (if the presser foot is in the up position, you can turn the dial all day long, and the tension won't change!) 3) When winding the bobbin, always thread the loose end of the thread through the hole in the side of the bobbin. If this loose thread end is held firmly, it will break off, leaving a smoothly wound supply of thread in your bobbin.

25 SEWING MACHINE ATTACHMENTS

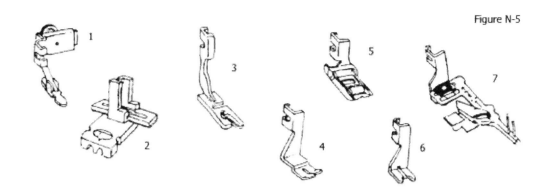

Figure N-5

1. <u>ZIPPER FOOT</u> - this foot is designed so that you can stitch very close to a raised edge like a zipper, or on cording.

2. <u>INVISIBLE ZIPPER FOOT</u> - this foot is designed to stitch an invisible zipper. This foot is usually adaptable to both the zipper and sewing machine style by means of plastic parts. (this is usually purchased separately from a notions supply department).

3. <u>HEMMING FOOT</u> - This foot is designed to form and stitch a perfect hem without basting or pressing in advance. It makes the small "shirt tail" type of hem. It is also used to attach ruffles, lace, or any decorative trim.

4. <u>GATHERING FOOT</u> - This foot is designed to lock uniform fullness into each stitch. It is to be used for shirring and gathering.

5. <u>ROLLER FOOT</u> - This foot is designed to feed hard-to-handle fabrics like nylon or vinyl without slipping.

6. <u>BUTTON FOOT</u> - This foot is designed to hold a 2 or 4-hole button firmly for zigzag or automatic stitching to secure it to the garment.

7. <u>BINDER FOOT</u> - This foot is designed to apply bias binding to an unfinished edge without pinning or basting in advance.

20348181R00060

Printed in Great Britain
by Amazon